# The Salem Witch Trials

**Carol Domblewski**

**SCHOLASTIC INC.**

New York   Toronto   London   Auckland   Sydney
Mexico City   New Delhi   Hong Kong   Buenos Aires

**Illustrations
Sally Wern Comport**

Text copyright © 2003 by Scholastic Inc.
Illustrations copyright © 2003 by Sally Wern Comport.
All rights reserved. Published by Scholastic Inc.
Printed in the U.S.A.

ISBN 0-439-59771-4

SCHOLASTIC, SCHOLASTIC ACTION, and associated logos and designs are trademarks and/or registered trademarks of Scholastic Inc.

LEXILE is a registered trademark of MetaMetrics, Inc.

1  2  3  4  5  6  7  8  9  10     23     12 11 10 09 08 07 06 05 04 03

# Contents

# Welcome to This Book

*Have you noticed how quickly gossip travels around school? Have you ever known anyone who got hurt by that gossip?*

In Salem Village, Massachusetts, in 1692, gossip turned deadly. A group of young girls called some people witches. Back then, anyone who was called a witch could be hanged. In one year, 150 people from a small town ended up in jail. And 25 of them died.

How did the madness finally end?

**Target Words** This book will take you back to Salem Village in 1692. It was a scary place. These words will help you understand why.

- **accuse:** to say or claim that someone has done something wrong

  *Many people in Salem Village were accused of being witches.*

- **evidence:** proof that can be used to show that something is true or false

  *People were found guilty of being witches without any real evidence.*

- **rumor:** information that may not be true but is repeated by many people

  *The rumor about witches spread quickly in Salem Village.*

**Reader Tips** Here's how to get the most out of this book:

- **Illustrations** As you read, look at the illustrations in this book. They will give you a feel for the time period, the characters, and the setting.

- **Fact/Opinion** The facts tell what happened in Salem during the witch trials. People's feelings and beliefs about witches are opinions.

# Salem Village, 1692

What happened in Salem Village might be hard to believe today. That's why it helps to know what life was like back then.

Salem Village was settled by Puritans. The Puritans left England during the 1600s. They wanted religious freedom.

The Puritans were very serious about their beliefs. They worked and prayed a lot. They struggled to have pure hearts. That was very important to them and they thought about it a lot.

But in America, the Puritans had lots of other problems to think about. They had to work from sunup to sundown to survive. And they were living on Native American land. Tribes often captured or killed the townspeople. Disease was another problem. Smallpox had recently killed many people in the area.

Puritans had a religious explanation for their troubles. They believed very strongly in the devil. And they said that he was a cause of their problems. Anyone who was thought to be helping him was in serious trouble.

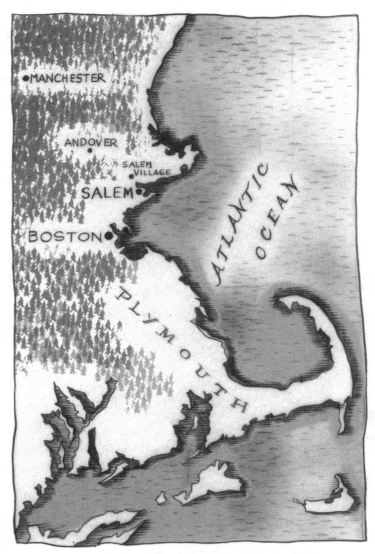

**This map shows Salem Village in the Bay Colony, 1692.**

# 1

# An Evil Hand

### *What was wrong with these girls?*

A deep forest grew at the edge of Salem Village. The tree branches looked like bony fingers. Cold winds blew. The days were short and the nights long. It was January 1692.

In the home of Reverend Samuel Parris, two girls had fallen ill. Betty Parris was 9. Her cousin Abigail Williams was 11. The girls twisted and turned. At moments, they seemed to choke. Sometimes their bodies grew stiff. They shouted crazy words. What were these strange fits? Were the girls about to die?

Reverend Parris was a very strict man. He made the girls work and pray. Now they were getting special attention. Was something really wrong with the girls? Or were they just pretending?

**Was something really wrong with Abigail and Betty?**

A month later the girls were still not better. Finally, the village doctor, William Griggs, came up with an answer. He said, "These children are under an evil hand."

**Rumors** spread through the village. The young girls were under the spell of witches! The Puritans believed that witches got special powers from the devil. They believed that witches could attack people and take over their bodies.

People **accused** of being witches were in serious trouble. If they were found guilty, they were hanged! This had just happened in Boston, a city fifteen miles away. Had the problem spread to Salem Village?

---**Heads Up!**---------------

*Look up* accused *in the glossary. How do you think people felt when they were accused of being witches?*

# 2

# Rumors

*The first three witches were named.*

The people of Salem Village wanted answers. They wanted names. So, the girls would have to say who the witches were. Or they would have to **admit** that they were lying. They named three women as witches.

Tituba was one of them. She worked for the Reverend Parris and his family as their slave. She was from the island of Barbados. Tituba followed a different religion. She believed in magic spells. She had told the girls many scary stories. She wore unusual clothes and spoke with an accent. The people of Salem Village thought Tituba was strange.

The second person accused was Sarah Osborne. She was also different. She was married to a much younger man. And he had

**Everyone was talking about witches.**

once worked for her! In 1692, **decent** women did not do such things. Some women would cross the road rather than walk near Sarah Osborne. They were afraid that her "evil" ways would rub off on them.

The third woman named was Sarah Good. Sarah Good smoked a pipe! And she was poor. Sometimes she begged for money. But she wasn't humble about it. She would yell at people if she thought they didn't give her enough. Sarah Good was also an **outcast** in Salem Village.

Once the women were named, the rumors spread around town like wildfire. Everyone was talking about the girls and the women they named as witches.

## Talk of the Town

"Did you hear about Betty Parris and Abigail Williams?" asked one older woman as she and

---**Heads Up!**---
*What did the women named as witches have in common? How were they different?*

her friend walked down the road. She leaned closer and whispered, "They are bewitched!"

The younger woman said a quick prayer.

But the older woman had even bigger news. She was dying to tell it. "More girls are having fits, too."

The younger woman shook her head and **gasped.** She didn't want to believe it. But she knew her friend would not lie.

"Oh, yes, there are witches here. Just like in Boston," said the older woman. "And the witches will hang. All three of them." And with that final statement, she smiled.

Her younger friend did not smile. She did not want to know who had been named as a witch. But **curiosity** got the better of her. "Who was named?" she finally asked.

The older woman's smile got bigger. "Tituba, the Indian slave of the Parris family, Sarah Osborne, and Sarah Good."

"Those poor women!" the younger woman cried. She knew Sarah Osborne and liked her. She did not think that she was a witch. And Tituba had strange ways but did not seem evil.

Sarah Good was just a poor old woman.

"Ha! Their being witches is no surprise to me!" her older friend cried.

**Heads Up!**

*Why do you think the older friend was not surprised by who was named as witches?*

# 3

## Fear Takes Over

***The witches went to trial.***

Witches seemed to be everywhere! More girls had fits. Neighbors began to **suspect** one another. Something had to be done. It was now March. The first three women named were arrested.

The accused were taken to the meeting house. They were going to be questioned. People whispered as they waited for the judges to start. The air crackled with excitement.

The first day of the **hearings** was like many days that would follow. The girls who had fits sat together. They were given a place of honor.

The judge called the first accused witch to come forward. Sarah Good slowly made her way to the front. She sat down. The whole town seemed to hold its breath.

The judge asked, "What evil spirit are you working with?"

"None," Sarah Good answered.

"Have you made a contract with the devil?"

"No."

"Why do you hurt these children?"

Sarah Good said, "I do not hurt them. I would never hurt them!"

"Who do you use to hurt them?"

Her voice cracked as she cried, "I don't use anybody!"

Sarah Good left quietly. She walked slowly, bent over and quiet. All her pride had left her.

## A Judge Lies

Next, the judge called Sarah Osborne. Sarah Osborne walked forward with her head held high. She felt she had nothing to fear.

The judge asked her many of the same questions. He began, "What evil spirit are you working with?"

Sarah Osborne answered, "None."

The judge asked, "Do you go around with Sarah Good?"

"I have not seen her in two years," Sarah Osborne said.

The judge went on, "Sarah Good said you hurt the children." But Sarah Good hadn't really said that. The judge just said so to get Sarah Osborne to **confess.**

But Sarah Osborne did not change her story. She said she never hurt the children. She also said she did not know the devil.

After the women were questioned, the judge turned back to the girls. He asked them to point to the witches. Everybody in the meeting house looked at the girls. The girls pointed at Sarah Good and Sarah Osborne. Then they fell into fits. People watched in horror. The girls cried that the spirit of Sarah Good was attacking them that very minute. Mothers clutched their children. They considered this **proof.**

## Tituba's Story

At first, Tituba denied working with evil spirits. But the Reverend Parris beat her for lying. When Tituba was questioned later, she

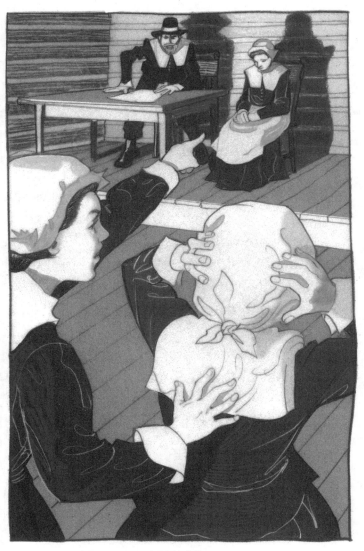

**The girls pointed and cried "Witch!"**

changed her story. She agreed that the devil was hurting the girls! The room went silent. Suddenly everyone was listening to her.

Tituba didn't disappoint her audience. She gave details about the devil. Sometimes he appeared like a hog or a dog. Sometimes he was a red cat, a yellow bird, or a white-haired man. She even said that she had talked with him!

Next, Tituba said she had ridden on "a stick or pole." She said that Sarah Good and Sarah Osborne were right behind her.

"Other witches hurt the children, too," Tituba finally stated.

People stared at their neighbors. They were very afraid.

That night some of the villagers thought they saw witches in the darkness. One woman said she felt a witch poke and pinch her. Tituba's story had taken their fear to a new level.

## Heads Up!

*Why do you think Tituba told that story during the trial?*

# 4

# A Good Woman or a Witch?

### *No one was safe.*

Three weeks later, some friends went to visit a kindly old woman. Her name was Rebecca Nurse. Everyone liked Rebecca. No one had ever said a bad word about her.

Rebecca said, "I've been so sick! But I've heard about what's happening. Those poor girls! I'm so sorry for them. I pray for them."

Rebecca's friends looked at each other. They did not know how to tell her. Finally, they just said it. "They say you are a witch too, Rebecca."

Rebecca Nurse was shocked. All she could do was shake her head. Who would accuse her? It turned out that many people named her as a witch, not just the young girls. They said her spirit attacked them. They said she had tried to make them sign the devil's book!

Rebecca cried out, "I am as innocent as an unborn child!" Then she said, "What have I done that God would punish me like this in my old age?"

At the end of March, Rebecca was brought in for questioning. The judge looked at the sweet, old woman. He asked her if she wanted to confess. If she did, she would not be hanged. But Rebecca shook her head. She was innocent. The judge sent her to jail. Witches could be anyone or anywhere.

## Heads Up!

*What do you think of Rebecca Nurse? Do you think the town was being fair to her? Why or why not?*

# 5

# A Deadly Mistake!

### *The girls were to be feared.*

Everyone in Salem Village liked John and Elizabeth Proctor. They were thought to be good people. One day, John Proctor's young servant, Mary Warren, said she saw a witch. She had a fit. She twisted and turned.

John was there at the time. He did not believe Mary. He told her she did not see a witch. It was just his shadow.

John was upset with Mary. He thought that she was playing a game just like the other girls. He did not believe in witches. He thought the rumors were nonsense. And he thought Mary and the other girls were lying.

So, he gave Mary extra work. He told her he would beat her if she had more fits. Mary Warren had more fits anyway.

**When John found out about Mary's fits, he was angry.**

When John found out, he could not stop his anger. "Those girls will make us all devils and witches!" he boomed.

## More Witches

In April, John Proctor's wife, Elizabeth, was arrested. People had named her as a witch. The next day, they named John as a witch, too.

Mary Warren was upset. She knew the Proctors weren't witches. Now they were in jail. Mary and the Proctor children were left all alone. The crops were dying. And people began to steal from the Proctor's house and farm.

## Mary Writes a Letter

Mary knew she had done something wrong. Her fits had caused the Proctors to be accused. She wanted to make it up to the Proctors. So she wrote a short note to her minister.

"The girls lied," was all it said.

**Heads Up!**
*Why did Mary want to stop the madness?*

The minister read it aloud at church. But her note did not stop the madness. Instead it made the girls and all the other **afflicted** people angry. And it scared them. If people didn't believe that they were being attacked by witches, they might be called witches themselves.

The next day, the girls had more fits. This time, they blamed Mary. When Mary heard that she was being called a witch, she **panicked.** She was young and alone—and scared. If they found her guilty of being a witch, they would hang her! There was only one thing left to do.

Mary changed her story back again. She had fits. She said that witches had taken over her body. She said that they had made her write the note. Mary was safe again.

## Another Step Forward

Soon, another villager called the girls liars. His name was Giles Corey. He was a loud man. And the Puritans did not like people who were loud. They especially did not like people who caused trouble. Giles Corey had been in trouble before. He didn't have many friends.

So, when Giles Corey called the girls liars, no one listened. Instead, they called him a witch, and threw him in jail. That was the final warning. No one would dare speak out now. Speaking out might mean death.

## Heads Up!

*What has happened now? How would you describe Salem?*

# 6

# Hang Them!

### *How did the madness end?*

More villagers were being jailed for witchcraft all the time. In jail they were told that if they confessed to being witches they would be safe. If they didn't confess, they were **tortured.** Still, hardly anyone confessed.

Something needed to be done. The Bay Colony (now Massachusetts) had just gotten a new governor, Sir William Phipps. And his first job was to deal with the accused witches.

Governor Phipps set up a special court for trying witches. Seven judges would hear the cases and decide.

People were hopeful. Maybe the new governor would be able to sort out the witches from the good people. Then Salem Village would be safe.

The trials began on June 2nd. Bridget Bishop was the first to be **convicted** as a witch. She was hanged eight days later on Gallows Hill. Many more hangings would follow.

For a moment it seemed that one person might have been found innocent. Rebecca Nurse took the stand. Nurse insisted that she was innocent. And she was such a beloved woman in the community. The jury believed her. They said she was innocent!

But then the judge asked the girls about Rebecca Nurse. The girls had fits. "Witch!" "Witch!" they cried, pointing at Rebecca. Could the old woman be making them suffer? It seemed so. The jury changed its mind. Rebecca was **sentenced** to death.

Rebecca Nurse, Sarah Good, and three others were hanged on July 19. On August 19, John Proctor and four others were hanged.

By September, over one hundred people were still in jail. All of them were accused of being witches.

Then Giles Corey's case came up. The court asked him to confess. But he refused. In fact,

**Many more hangings would follow before the madness was over.**

he refused to say anything at all. This made the court so angry that they decided to make him confess. He was forced to lie on a plank. Heavy stones were placed on his chest. Still, he wouldn't confess. They loaded on more stones. He was slowly being crushed to death. It took two days for him to die. He never confessed.

## The Last Straw

By October, 20 people had been put to death. It seemed as if the madness would never end. But there was hope.

Two important men spoke out against the trials. One was Increase Mather. He said, "It were better that ten suspected witches escape, than one innocent person should be **condemned.**"

---

**Heads Up!**

*In 1692, about 500 people lived in Salem Village. So having over 100 people in jail was a lot.*

---

The other man was Thomas Brattle. He sent a letter to the governor. In it, he said it was wrong to accuse people without real **evidence.**

But the real change came when someone accused Governor Phipps's own wife of witchcraft. Governor Phipps knew that his wife was not a witch. On October 29, the governor shut down the witch trials. No more people would be hanged. Three weeks later, the governor put a stop to all new arrests. But many were still in jail. Things were still far from normal.

## Heads Up!

*Thomas Brattle said that it was wrong to accuse people without evidence. Is that a fact or opinion?*

*And they all lived sadly ever after.*

A year had gone by from the time Abigail and Betty had their first fits. During that time nineteen people had been hanged. One had died by torture. Five others, including a baby, died in jail. Even two dogs had been tried as witches and killed.

In May of 1693, a new trial took place with new rules for evidence. No one else was convicted. Those still in jail were freed. Tituba was released, but she was sold to a new master.

In 1697, Massachusetts held a special day for remembering. Prayers were said for the people who had been put to death with no real proof. One of the judges and all twelve members of the jury publicly apologized. They asked forgiveness from God. They also asked the families of the accused to forgive them.

Many families had lost their farms. They never got back their wealth or respect. Later, the government paid money to the families of those who had been killed.

Today, people still look back on the witch trials with sadness. In 1957 and again in 2001, leaders of Massachusetts apologized. But are those apologies enough?

The memory of the witch trials still falls across Salem Village like a shadow.

---**Heads Up!**---

*What do you think about what happened in Salem Village? What would you have done if you lived then? Use the facts you learned to support your answer.*

**Twenty-five people died as a result of the Salem witch trials.**

# Glossary

**accuse** *(verb)* to say or claim that someone has done something wrong (p. 10)

**admit** *(verb)* to say that you did something wrong (p. 11)

**afflicted** *(adjective)* suffering pain or harm (p. 26)

**confess** *(verb)* to admit to doing something wrong (p. 18)

**convict** *(verb)* to find guilty of a crime by a court (p. 29)

**condemn** *(verb)* to find guilty and give the punishment of death (p. 31)

**curiosity** *(noun)* a strong interest to know more about something (p. 14)

**decent** *(adjective)* respectable and good (p. 13)

**evidence** *(noun)* proof that can be used to show something is true or false (p. 32)

**gasp** *(verb)* to take in a breath of air to show surprise (p. 14)

**hearing** *(noun)* a formal question-and-answer session (p. 16)

**outcast** *(noun)* someone who is not part of the group (p. 13)

**panic** *(verb)* to be affected by extreme fear (p. 26)

**proof** *(noun)* facts or evidence that something is true (p. 18)

**rumor** *(noun)* information that may not be true but is repeated by many people (p. 10)

**sentence** *(verb)* to give a punishment, often jail or death (p. 29)

**suspect** *(verb)* to think or believe something without proof (p. 16)

**torture** *(noun)* using extreme pain to force someone to say or do something (p. 28)

# Index

# Index